P9-BYT-175

GUIDE TO
MEXICO

BRIAN WILLIAMS

Highlights for Children

CONTENTS

On the cover:
  The Pyramid of Kukulcán, at the heart of Chichén Itzá, Mexico, is the largest pyramid ever built.

Published by Highlights for Children
© 1995 Highlights for Children, Inc.

All rights reserved. No part of this book may be reproduced or transmitted in any form or by any means, electronic or mechanical, including photocopying, recording, or by any information storage and retrieval system, without permission in writing from the publisher.

10 9 10 11 12 13 14 15

ISBN 0-87534-912-9

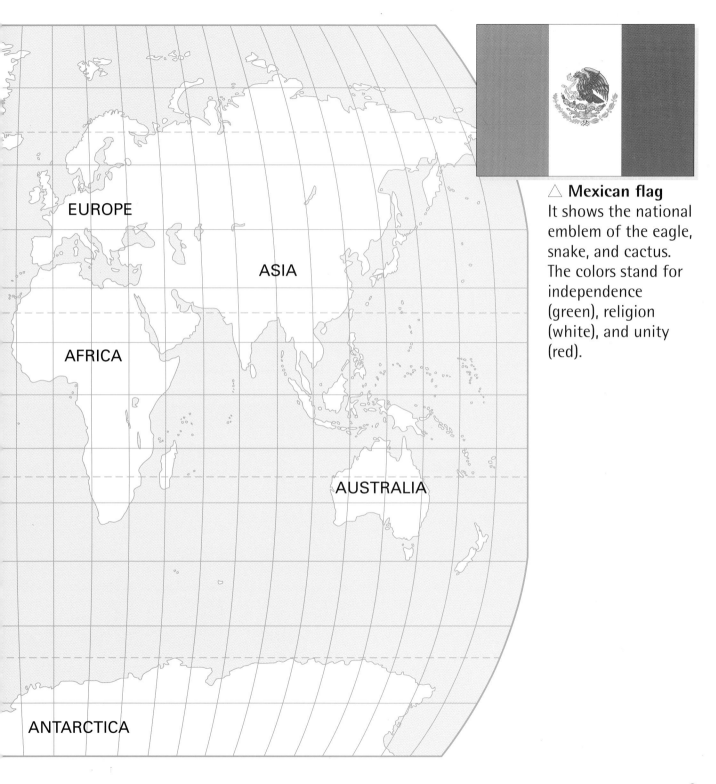

EUROPE

ASIA

AFRICA

AUSTRALIA

ANTARCTICA

△ **Mexican flag**
It shows the national
emblem of the eagle,
snake, and cactus.
The colors stand for
independence
(green), religion
(white), and unity
(red).

MEXICO AT A GLANCE

Area 756,198 square miles (1,958,201 square kilometers)

Population 89,955,000

Capital Mexico City, population of the city and surroundings 20,000,000

Other big cities Guadalajara (population 2,847,000), Monterrey (2,522,000), Puebla (1,054,000)

Highest mountain Citlaltépetl, 18,701 feet (5,667 meters)

Longest river Rio Grande 1,550 miles (2,480 kilometers) within Mexico

Largest lake Lake Chapala, 417 square miles (1,080 square kilometers)

Official language Spanish

▽ **Mexican stamps** Some show common Mexican plants, Latin American flags, and the Mexican Grand Prix car race course. Others honor Columbus's historic voyage and Simon Bolivar, hero of Latin America.

▷ **Mexican money**
Mexico's currency is the new peso. The sign is like the U.S. dollar sign ($). Peso notes of 10, 20, 50, 100, 200, and 500 are available. One new peso equals 100 centavos.

UNITED STATES
OF AMERICA

© Oxford Cartographers

MEXICO

Farmland & Forest
Desert

0 50 100 150 200 Miles
0 100 200 300 Kilometers

★ Capital
● Major Cities
▲ Mountain Peaks
∴ Ancient Ruin
— Country Boundary

Sierra

Yaqui

• Cananea

Chihuahua •

Copper
Canyon

Sierra Tarahumara

• Los
Mochis

Rio Grande

Rio
Bravo

Monterrey •

Gulf of
Mexico

of California

Durango •

• Rio
Grande

Cabo San
Lucas

Zacatecas •

• Guadalupe

• Tabasco

León •

Tampico •

Puerto
Vallarta •

Guadalajara •

Lake
Chapala

M
a
d
r
e

Pachuca •

**Mexico
City** ★
Rio Hondo • ★

Teotihuacán ∴

Nevado de Toluca ▲
Popocatépetl ▲

▲ Puebla •

Balsas

Citlaltépetl ▲

• Veracruz

Chichén
Itzá ∴

Uxmal ∴

Campeche •

Y u c a t á n

Palenque •

BELIZE

Acapulco •

Oaxaca •
▲

• Chiapa

GUATEMALA

HONDURAS

P A C I F I C   O C E A N

Tapachula •

EL
SALVADOR

105°W   100°W   95°W   90°W

5

WELCOME TO MEXICO

Mexico is a big country with a large population. Mexico is three times the size of Texas. It has more people than any country in the Americas other than the United States and Brazil. Mexico lies just south of the United States. Its longest river, the Río Bravo, or Rio Grande, forms much of the border between the two countries.

Mexico is a country of color and variety. This is true of its climate, land, and people. Here you will find hot deserts, snowy mountains, volcanoes, grassy plains, and tropical rain forests. Many Mexicans live in small villages, far from the nearest town. Yet the capital, Mexico City, is the world's biggest city. Among its crowded streets, modern skyscrapers tower over ancient temples.

Mexico was once the land of the Maya, Aztec, Zatopec, and other tribes. Today it is a thriving nation with factories, oil wells, modern cities, and farms. Welcome to Mexico.

▽ **A country church** In the distance is Iztaccíhuatl (an Aztec word for "white woman"), a snow-capped volcano 17,442 feet (5,286 meters) high.

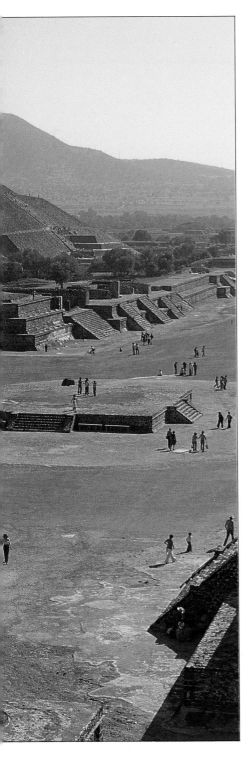

◁ **The Pyramid of the Sun at Teotihuacán** The pyramid-temple is 218 feet (66 meters) high.

△ **Girls in holiday clothes** Children under the age of 18 make up about 50 percent of Mexico's population.

Today almost all Mexicans speak Spanish. But most of the country's population are *mestizos*, people of mixed Spanish and Indian origins. Many believe the first people came to Mexico more than 20,000 years ago. They were hunters and farmers, living in villages. Later they built great cities like Teotihuacán with its huge stone pyramids. You can visit the remains of this 2,000-year-old city today, 33 miles (50 kilometers) north of Mexico City.

In the early 1500s, Spanish explorers sailed from Europe to Mexico. As they made their way through the country, they gained control of many native tribes. The Spanish brought their language and their Catholic religion. Many Mexicans remain proud of their native heritage.

MEXICO CITY

Many visitors travel first to the capital, Mexico City. It lies in a valley at the southern end of Mexico's two main high mountain chains, the Sierra Madre ranges.

Mexico City is 7,575 feet (2,295 meters) above sea level. Visitors may need a few days to get used to breathing the thin air. This is a big city. You will need time to explore its *avenidas* (avenues) and *plazas* (squares). Take a bus or taxi to travel along the Paseo de la Reforma. The city's most famous avenues are lined with tall buildings. As you journey through the city, you can admire the monuments to Mexican heroes. Other attractions include the wall paintings, or murals, of famous artists like Diego Rivera and José Clemente Orozco.

▽ **A view over Mexico City** The city streets are laid out in blocks. To the left is the Palace of Fine Arts, a theater and museum built in the 19th century. It stands beside the central park, La Alameda.

▽ **The Floating Gardens of Xochimilco** People come here to take boat trips and stroll by the canals.

In Mexico City, buses with odd route numbers run north and south. Buses with even numbers go east and west. You can travel underground, too, on subway trains that are fast and comfortable. But watch out for the morning, lunchtime, and evening rush hours. At Pino Suárez subway station you will find yourself in a restored Aztec temple.

Above ground, the city streets are jammed with traffic. This adds to the air pollution problem. The mountains around Mexico City trap the smoke and gases from cars, factories, and buildings. The build-up of fumes causes a blanket of smog that can make your eyes and throat hurt.

About 19 million people live in Mexico City and its suburbs. Some families can afford modern apartments and homes. Many others live in shacks in the city's poorer areas.

▽ **A city cab** Taxis like this yellow Volkswagen are being replaced by green ones that use unleaded gas.

LAND OF THE AZTECS

Mexico City stands on the ruins of a city called Tenochtitlán. It was built more than 600 years ago by the Aztecs. These mighty people ruled an empire in Mexico.

Next to the Aztec ruins are many modern buildings, such as the Latin American Tower. It is 44 stories high and has special underground supports to protect it from earthquakes. In 1985, an earthquake struck the city, killing thousands of people.

Today's main city square, the Zócalo, is alive with people. It is also exactly where the Aztecs gathered for ceremonies and other activities. Around the Zócalo are Aztec ruins, Spanish-style palaces, and the great Cathedral. The National Palace, at the east end of the Zócalo, is where Mexico's president works. Visitors admire the beauty of the building itself and the magnificent murals inside.

△ **Guadalupe Day celebrations** December 12 honors the Virgin of Guadalupe, Mexico's patron saint. Some people wear Aztec costumes.

◁ **Aztec stone figures** These statues, made in the 1400s, are from the Great Temple of Tenochtitlán.

From Mexico City on a rare clear day you may see Popocatépetl. In the Aztec language this name means "the smoking mountain." Near a lake in the shadow of this volcano, the Aztecs founded their city of Tenochtitlán around 1345. From here, they ruled an empire of about 10 million people. In 1521, the Spanish arrived. The great Aztec emperor, Montezuma, was killed and Tenochtitlán was nearly destroyed. The Spaniards built Christian churches over Aztec temples. Many churches show angels and Indian symbols in a blend of cultures.

Workers digging near the Zócalo in 1978 found the remains of the main Aztec pyramid, called the Great Temple. You can visit this site where many Aztec treasures have been dug up.

A bus ride westward along the Paseo de la Reforma takes you to Chapultepec Park. Aztec emperors once relaxed here. Now there are museums, picnic areas, and a zoo. You can buy souvenirs in stores and markets. Mexicans love markets. For crafts such as leatherwork, visit the San Juan market.

◁ **A spectacular view of Popocatépetl** This volcano erupted in 1802, and smoke is often seen rising from its heights.

FONDAS AND BULLFIGHTS

Mexicans enjoy food. In any town or city, you will find freshly cooked dishes that will make your mouth water. You can eat at a *fonda* (small restuarant), where food is inexpensive. Small restaurants and food stalls are often family businesses. Everyone lends a hand, including children.

Mexican cooking mixes native and Spanish styles. Among the foods Mexico has given the world are tomatoes, avocados, and chocolate. Meat dishes flavored with sauces are very popular. Other common foods include corn tortillas, beans, rice, and chili.

For some Mexicans, lunch is a quick *taco* or a *torta* (sandwich). But many people eat the main meal of the day at about two o'clock in the afternoon. The meal consists of several courses; the drink is usually water blended with juice.

The best way to travel to towns near Mexico City is by bus or train. You will notice that most Mexicans wear modern clothes. However, you may see some people in the more traditional dress of a *sombrero* (wide-brimmed hat) and a *poncho* (blanket with a hole for the head).

You are very likely to see people headed to a bullfight. There are more than 700 bullfighting arenas in Mexico. If you do not like bullfights, try a soccer match at the famous Aztec Stadium in Mexico City.

For a trip in the countryside, people often drive from Mexico City along the "road of a thousand peaks." This takes them through mountain scenery and small, peaceful towns. Many people visit Lake Pátzcuaro, where fishermen catch fish in butterfly-shaped nets.

△ **A food stall** The owner is making *tortillas*. These cornmeal pancakes can be eaten plain or filled with meat, cheese, or beans.

◁ **Fishermen on Lake Pátzcuaro** The fishermen dip their nets into the water, then lift them out carefully. They sell the fish at market.

▷ **Plaza de Toros Mexico in Mexico City** This is the world's largest bullring, with seats for 50,000 spectators. Bullfighting was introduced from Spain in the 1520s.

SILVER MINES AND CLIFF DIVERS

On weekends, cars jam the roads leading south out of Mexico City as people visit the countryside. Many drivers head first for the town of Cuernavaca. From here, the main road runs through the small state of Morelos. This area is best known for growing sugarcane. The revolutionary leader, Emiliano Zapata, was born here. He died in 1919 but is still a local hero.

A little farther south is the pretty town of Taxco. Its narrow streets and small, red-roofed houses are a reminder of what Mexico was like during Spanish rule. Since that time, Taxco has been an important silver mining center. Metals are still mined in the nearby hills. In Taxco's shops and markets, tourists can buy beautiful crafts made of silver and copper.

▽ **Tarascan Indians** These people come from an area west of Mexico City. Copperware that they make is sold in village markets. Buyers and sellers bargain over prices.

▽ Cliff divers of Acapulco
Their leaps from the cliff top into the ocean require much courage and skill.

▽ Farmers harvest corn near Acapulco Tourists come and go, but the work of the farm goes on through the seasons.

The road south takes you to the warm, tropical coast and the Pacific Ocean. The biggest town here is Acapulco. In the 1500s, Spanish sailing ships stopped in Acapulco Bay for supplies on their long journeys to the Far East. Today, planes jet in to Acapulco's airport from all over the world, bringing visitors to Mexico's biggest tourist resort.

Winter is the busiest season in Acapulco. Visitors from cold-weather countries fill its hotels. They come to enjoy sandy beaches, golf courses, and deep-sea fishing. Tourists marvel at the daring high divers who leap 150 feet (45 meters) off the cliffs of La Quebrada.

Foreign visitors fly to Acapulco, but most Mexicans travel here by car or bus. First-class buses are fast and air-conditioned. Other buses provide a more leisurely journey but are often crowded. Travelers on buses like to eat and drink and chat with their neighbors.

JUNGLES AND OILWELLS

As you travel from Mexico City to the town of Puebla, you pass factories making cars, chemicals, clothing, electrical goods, and other products. Puebla is a busy state capital with elegant Spanish-style buildings. The town's cathedral was finished in 1649.

From Puebla, a railroad runs to another state capital, Oaxaca. It is a short drive from Oaxaca to the mountaintop temples of Monte Alban. These pyramids were built by the Zapotec people more than 1,000 years ago. Two of Mexico's presidents, Benito Juárez and Porfirio Díaz, came from this region.

North of Oaxaca and toward the Gulf of Mexico is Citlaltépetl, or Pico de Orizaba. This is Mexico's highest mountain. The gulf coast is flat and has many lagoons and rivers flowing through it. In places there is thick rain forest. The busiest port on the gulf is Veracruz. Here ships load rubber, lumber, sugar, chemicals, and oil products for export.

The states of Veracruz, Campeche, and Tabasco are oil-producing regions of Mexico. Here you will see derricks and oil refineries. Out in the gulf, huge oil rigs drill for oil under the ocean floor.

◁ **An Indian weaver**
Weavers use traditional-color dyes and patterns, and each region of Mexico has its own design styles. Selling woven goods, such as shawls and blankets, adds to a family's income. Women cover their heads with woven shawls called *rebozos.*

16

▽ **An oil rig in the Gulf of Mexico**
Mexico has more oil than any other country in Latin America. Oil sales to other countries make up 60 percent of Mexico's exports.

▽ **A jaguar in the Tabasco rain forest** A few jaguars still hunt in the swamps. Ancient Mexicans, the Olmecs, worshiped this spotted cat, which is now becoming rare.

At La Venta Park Museum in Tabasco, you can see giant stone heads carved by the Olmecs. These people lived along the gulf coast from 1200 to 400 B.C.

South of Tabasco is the state of Chiapas. This was the land of the Mayas, who built a great civilization more than 1,000 years ago. At the ancient site of Palenque, you can see Maya temples and palaces.

In this southeast part of Mexico there are mainly dirt roads. A sturdy truck is the best way to get around the region. And you will need waterproof clothes, because the jungle is soaked by as much as 10 feet (300 centimeters) of rain a year.

MAYA MARVELS OF YUCATÁN

Yucatán is the easternmost part of Mexico. The land here is flat and the climate is hot. Local people wear loose cotton clothes to keep cool. They often sleep outdoors in hammocks. You may see hammock sellers in the street.

Yucatán was hard to explore before modern highways were built. Now you can journey by car or bus to see the ruins at Uxmal. Here the Mayans built stone temples and palaces. One unusual rounded pyramid is called the Pyramid of the Magician. Mexicans will tell you it was made by a dwarf, using magic!

△ **The Chacmool, or messenger of the gods** This fearsome ancient stone figure is from Chichén Itzá. On its stomach is a space for sacrificial offerings.

▷ **The beach at Cozumel Island** You can go sightseeing in a glass-bottomed boat or dive underwater to look at fish and coral.

18

The main city of Yucatán is Mérida. It is known for the trees and other plants that grow there. A local plant, *sisal*, has long fibers that are twisted together to make rope. People even wear hats made from sisal. Sapodilla trees grow nearby in the tropical forests. These trees are tapped for *chicle*, a liquid used to make chewing gum. *Cacao*, the plant from which chocolate is made, also grows in this region.

It is a three-hour bus trip from Merida to Chichén Itzá. Here you can peer into a mysterious sacred well, which is a natural, flooded pit in the soft rock. The Mayans threw treasures and human victims into the well as sacrifices to their gods. You can also see a Toltec ball court. Games played on the ball court were similar to present day ball games.

On the Caribbean coast, you can enjoy water sports or relax on the white sands of Cancún. Pirates once hid out on the nearby island of Cozumel. It is now a paradise for scuba and deep-sea divers, who swim in the warm, clear waters of the world's second biggest coral reef.

▽ **A school class in Mérida** Children learn about their country's past and today's world.

MUSIC AND RODEOS

You can travel by train from Mérida back to Mexico City and westward to Guadalajara. From a train window, you can enjoy the rugged scenery of central Mexico. There are mountains, dusty plains, and lakes.

▽ **Guadalajara's cathedral** This building is a beautiful mixture of architectural styles. It was begun in 1558.

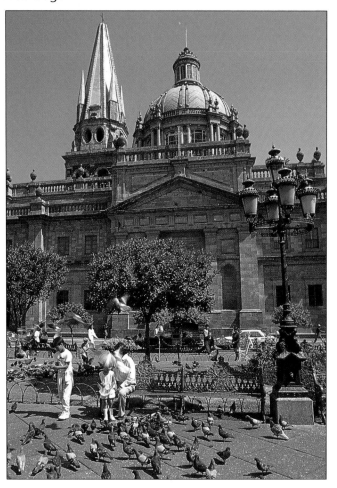

Guadalajara is Mexico's second biggest city and the capital of Jalisco State. At the center of Guadalajara are a magnificent cathedral and the state governor's palace. The city has grown quickly, with factories making textiles, shoes, and chemicals. In its busy market, you can bargain with the traders. About 50 miles (80 kilometers) southeast from Guadalajara is Lake Chapala. It is the largest lake in Mexico.

Jalisco is the home of *mariachi* street musicians. These are bands of trumpeters, guitarists, violinists, and singers. They play lively, rhythmic music that will make you want to tap your feet. The proud people of Jalisco call themselves *tapatíos*, which means, "I am three times better than you!"

In Jalisco you are likely to see Mexican cowboys. Central Mexico has dairy cattle. Ranges for the country's beef cattle are farther north. Mexican cowboys are called *charros*. You will hear stories and songs about their adventures. And if you visit a country *charreada*, or rodeo, you will be thrilled by the cowboys' skill on horseback. A *charro* can throw a bull by grabbing its tail, or by roping its legs. He can also ride a bucking bronco, or wild horse.

▷ **A country charreada** Cowboys still take part in these Mexican-style rodeos. They wear leather *chaps* over their pants to protect their legs from thorny bushes.

▷ **Plowing with horses** In Mexico there are still some farms where tractors are not used. Huge estates formerly owned by rich landowners have been divided into many small farms.

HEROES AND SAINTS

East of Guadalajara is the small town of Dolores Hidalgo. Here, in 1810, a priest named Father Miguel Hidalgo called on Mexican people to end Spanish rule. Hidalgo led a peasant army. He was captured and killed by government forces in 1811. Independence Day, September 16, honors Father Hidalgo's cry for freedom.

On December 12, crowds of churchgoers celebrate the Day of the Virgin of Guadalupe. This is an important religious holiday when Catholics celebrate the Virgin Mary's appearance to a native Mexican in 1536. The Basilica of Guadalupe, big enough to hold 10,000 people, now stands on the site of the vision. Pilgrims come to this shrine, sometimes finishing the journey on their knees in prayer. You see pictures of *La Virgen Morena* (the Brown Madonna) in cabs, buses, and cafés all over the city.

Mexicans call joyful holidays *fiestas*. People put on their best clothes and have fun. They eat, dance, and set off fireworks. On December 25 Mexicans celebrate Christmas, and on January 6 the "three kings" bring gifts to children. Blindfolded children use sticks to try to break *piñatas*, which are figures made from paper or clay covered with colorful paper. The *piñatas* are filled with candy, fruit, or toys.

February or March marks the start of Lent. This is a season of prayer and fasting leading up to Easter. In the week before Lent, some people celebrate Carnival with parades and parties. November 1 is All Souls' Day, and November 2 is the Day of the Dead, when people visit family graves. Children dress in costumes, and cooks make skulls and skeletons out of candy and pastry for the children to eat. This a fun holiday based on special ancient traditions.

▷ **Feathered costumes** Brightly colored clothes and pictures of the Virgin are seen at Guadalupe Day parades.

△ **Fiesta time** Mexicans have many fiestas during the year. Here, drummers and dancers mingle with churchgoers.

▽ **Children dressed as witches** The Day of the Dead is a holiday similar to Halloween. Mexicans often cook the favorite foods of their dead relatives and visit their graves.

A Fabulous Railroad

The northeast part of Mexico is hot and dry. Here, day temperatures often stay above 86°F (30°C) all summer long. In the 1590s, Spanish explorers came to this region looking for silver. They founded the famous silver mines of San Luis Potosí.

From the silver mines, the main road leads to Monterrey, Mexico's third biggest city and a major industrial center. All around, smoke rises into the sky from steelwork plants and factories where pottery, glass, and textiles are produced.

A trip from Monterrey to Chihuahua City takes all day by bus, or just an hour by plane. The state of Chihuahua is famous for the tiny breed of dog of the same name. In Chihuahua City you can visit a museum honoring Pancho Villa. This famous bandit and general is a national hero. He was a champion of poor people during the Revolution of 1910.

From Chihuahua, you should not miss the train ride east to the Pacific coast. The mountain railroad to Los Mochis near the coast was begun in 1898, but took 60 years to finish. A single-track line twists and climbs through the spectacular scenery of the Sierra Madre mountains. The railroad is an amazing engineering feat.

There are 86 tunnels and 39 bridges in the last 100 miles (160 kilometers) of track.

You can get off the train to look down into the Copper Canyon, more than 4,000 feet (1,212 meters) deep. At the train stop, you will see Tarahumara Indians. They are famous for running races that last as long as three days and nights!

△ **A family meal** Eating together is part of Mexican family life. Northern Mexicans enjoy Chihuahua's cheese soup and Monterrey's grilled goat meat called *cabrito*.

24

◁ **A train stop on the Copper Canyon railroad** Indians come to the train stop to sell food, dolls, and woven baskets. Before the railroad was built, these people had little contact with the outside world.

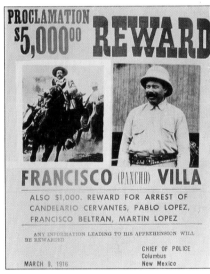

△ **An old "Wanted" poster** It offers a reward for the capture of Pancho Villa, a famous military leader and bandit. Villa tried to help people who did not have good homes or enough food.

25

DESERT MEETS OCEAN

After leaving the railroad at Los Mochis, take the bus south to Mazatlán. The trip takes seven hours along the coast highway. Mazatlán is the biggest port on Mexico's west coast. Here you can eat shrimp and fish fresh from the sea. Swimmers must take care, though, for this part of the ocean is deep, and the waves and currents can be dangerous.

Three rivers — the Colorado, Yaqui, and Fuerte — flow west from the Sierra Madre mountains to the sea. Farmers take water from the rivers to irrigate their crops of tomatoes, rice, cotton, vegetables, and sugarcane. In some areas, coffee plants are also grown.

▷ **Cattle on a ranch in Baja California** Ranching is very important in northern Mexico. Mexico has more than 30 million cattle, about one-third as many as the United States.

△ **A mariachi band** These musicians originally played at weddings. They sing and play guitars, violins, and trumpets.

◁ **Children choose comics** Although Mexicans are proud of their ancient traditions and customs, the modern culture of the United States has a strong influence here.

26

From Mazatlán, a ferry boat crosses the Gulf of California to the port of La Paz in Baja California. This is a long narrow peninsula, which looks like an arm, on Mexico's west side. The climate in Baja California is hot and dry. Cactus plants in the desert grow more than 66 feet (20 meters) tall.

Baja in Spanish means "lower." Near Mexicali in the far north of Baja California is the lowest point in Mexico. It is 33 feet (10 meters) below sea level. Most of Baja's people live around Mexicali, where farms are watered by irrigation.

From January to March, you can take boats from ports along the west coast to watch gray whales in the ocean around Scammon Lagoon. The whales swim south from Alaska, a journey of 5,000 miles (8,000 kilometers), to give birth to their young.

Baja California used to have few main roads and few visitors. Now you can travel on a modern highway from south to north, and to the U.S. border. The border town of Tijuana is the first place that many North American visitors see of Mexico. This bustling town is best known for its horse races and brass bands.

MEXICO FACTS AND FIGURES

The exciting Totonac Fliers The team captain on top of the pole represents the sun. The four fliers circle around him 13 times each, while hanging upside down.

People

Most Mexicans are *mestizos*, of mixed European and American Indian origins. Their European ancestors were mostly 16th-century Spanish conquerors and settlers. About 50 different groups of Indians live in Mexico. Some Mexicans have Black ancestry; Africans were brought to the country as slaves in colonial times.

Trade and industry

Oil, natural gas, and oil products are Mexico's most valuable exports. Oil is found offshore and underneath the rocks of the eastern states of Campeche, Tabasco, and Veracruz. Despite its oil wealth, Mexico is not a rich country.

Mexico's industries produce vehicles, steel, machinery, chemicals, and fertilizers. From mines come gold, silver, copper, lead, manganese, salt, sulfur, and zinc. Mexico is the world's leading supplier of silver.

Tourism is important. About 6 million tourists come to Mexico every year, mainly from the U.S.A.

Fishing

Mexicans catch great quantities of fish in lakes and rivers and from the ocean. Anchovies, oysters, shrimp, tuna, and sardines are netted along the Pacific and gulf coasts. Deep-sea fishing is a popular sport. People catch marlin and other game fish.

Farming

Only about one-eighth of Mexico is suitable for growing crops. Most of the land is too dry, too mountainous, or too swampy. Mexican farmers grow mainly corn — and about 50 kinds of beans. Other crops include rice, bananas, coffee, cotton, sugarcane, tomatoes, wheat, and chili peppers. Tropical fruits, such as mangoes and pineapples, grow well. Sisal, cacao, and vanilla plants are also grown.

Cattle are raised for dairy products and beef. Most farms are small communal farms run by local farmers.

Food

Mexican food is a mixture of Indian and Spanish. Corn is the most important crop. People soak corn cobs in water, then remove, boil, and grind the corn kernels into cornmeal. They bake the meal into *tortillas*, pancakes cooked on a griddle. *Frijoles* (beans) are eaten boiled, mashed, and then fried, often with tortillas. Rice is another basic food.

Most Mexicans like their food flavored with hot chili peppers. *Mole* is a popular sauce, which has chocolate, spices, and peppers in it.

Some other popular dishes :
tacos: folded tortillas with a variety of fillings
enchiladas: filled, rolled-up tortillas, covered with a mild or spicy sauce
tostadas: tortillas fried until crisp, served with beans, meat, or cheese
atole: a souplike corn dish
tamales: ground, spicy meat rolled in cornmeal dough, wrapped in banana leaves or corn husks, and steamed.
Coffee is a popular drink.

Schools
All Mexican children from the age of 6 through 14 must go to school . After six years of elementary school, children go on to three years of basic secondary school. Students graduating from these schools may go to upper secondary schools. From there, students can go on to college.

Although almost all Mexican children start school, only about one-half finish elementary school.

Toltec stone warrior At the Temple of the Morning Star at Tula, the Toltec capital, there are four stone warriors. Each is 15 feet (4.5 meters) tall.

The Media
Television is broadcast by two stations, TV Azteca and Televisa. All TV broadcasts are in Spanish. There are many radio stations.

Mexico has more than 300 daily newspapers and about 100 magazines. Leading newspapers include *Le Prensa, Esta, Novedadas,*

and *El Excélsior*, which are all published in Mexico City. Most of the leading newspapers and magazines are published in Spanish.

Art
Murals, or wall paintings, are a famous part of Mexican Indian art. The Mayas painted on walls, and modern Mexican mural painters, such as Diego Rivera (1886-1957), have continued this traditional style of painting. Often these paintings are very large and colorful. They show scenes of peasant life or events from Mexico's history, especially the revolution.

Music
Traditional music includes *corridos,* or folksongs, *mariachi* bands, and tunes played on the *marimba,* an instrument like a xylophone with wooden keys. Four persons — often the members of one family — play the marimba together.

Ancient Indian musical instruments include the *huehuetl,* a log drum, and clay flutes and whistles. Folk dances are also popular.

MEXICO FACTS AND FIGURES

Religion

Almost all Mexicans are Roman Catholics. The law grants freedom of worship for all, but the Church is asked not to take part in politics.

Christianity was introduced to Mexico by the Spanish in the 1500s. Priests and missionaries converted the Indians. But many people still hold on to old beliefs.

Festivals and holidays

Below are some of the many national holidays in Mexico.

January 6 **Three Kings Day**
A day for giving Christmas gifts, especially to children

March 21 **Birthday of Benito Juárez**

September 16 **Independence Day**

November 2 **The Day of the Dead** People visit family graves and eat candies shaped like skulls and skeletons.

December 12 **Day of the Virgin of Guadalupe** The main religious holiday, honoring the appearance of the Virgin Mary to a native Mexican in 1536

December 25 **Christmas Day**
This is called *Navidad* in Spanish.

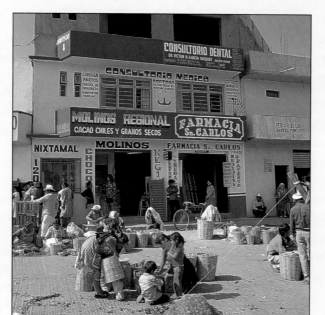

A town market in Oaxaca People bring their goods to sell in the dusty town square. Mexicans shop at the local stores, too.

Plants

Forest trees include valuable lumber species, such as ebony, rosewood, mahogany, and pine. From sapodilla trees people tap the gummy sap called *chicle,* which is used to make chewing gum. The maguey is a plant with fleshy leaves that can grow taller than a person. The juice from its leaves is squeezed out to make drinks. From sisal plants rope is made.

Mexico has many beautiful flowers, including azaleas, orchids, and those of desert cactus plants. Some of its rain forest plants are grown as houseplants.

Animals

Large animals include mountain lions, deer, coyotes, jaguars, ocelots, alligators, and snakes. Among colorful birds of the warm forests are quetzals, macaws, and parrots. The tropical rain forests are home to armadillos, iguanas, fruit bats, tree frogs, and all kinds of insects, worms, and spiders.

Sport

Mexico's most popular sport is *futbol*, or soccer. The national soccer team is supported with great enthusiasm, and Mexico has hosted the World Cup, an international tournament that determines the champion.

Mexicans are keen fans of baseball, track and field sports, basketball, and *jai alai*, a fast ball court game. Bullfights attract noisy crowds in the cities, and local *charreadas*, or rodeos, are popular. Mexican boxers have won many professional world titles.

Tourists enjoy watersports and excellent game fishing at coastal resorts. Enthusiasts can go scuba diving among the coral reefs off the gulf coast.

History

People first lived in Mexico more than 20,000 years ago. Between 1200 and 400 B.C., the Olmecs developed a civilization along the gulf coast. From A.D. 250 to 1000 was the age of the Maya and Zapotecs. The Toltecs ruled an empire from the 900s A.D. They introduced the worship of the plumed serpent-god, Quetzalcóatl.

The Aztecs were the last of the empire builders of Mexico. They built Tenochtitlán, a city of 100,000 people. They were traders and farmers.

Europeans knew nothing of these empires before Columbus sailed from Spain to the New World in 1492. Spanish sailors and soldiers came to Mexico in the 1500s. By 1521 the soldier Hernán Cortés gained control of Mexico for the Spanish. The Aztecs and other ancient Indian tribes lost power and much of their civilization was destroyed. But through the ages people have clung to many customs and beliefs. Spain ruled Mexico until 1821, when Mexico gained its independence as a republic.

During wars with Texas (1836) and the United States (1848), Mexico lost much of its northern territory. After these setbacks, the country recovered under a great president, Benito Juárez. From 1876, Mexico was ruled by the dictator Porfirio Díaz. He was overthrown by a revolution in 1911.

Modern Mexico has economic problems despite many natural resources and steadily growing oil wealth. Mexico's population continues to grow fast, and many of its people remain poor.

Language

Mexico has more people who speak Spanish than any other country in the world. Nearly all Mexicans speak Spanish. Most Indians speak their own languages as well as Spanish. There are 58 Indian languages spoken in Mexico. They include Mayan, Mixtec, Tarascan, and Zapotec. Many place names in Mexico are Indian, like the name of the country itself. English is widely understood, especially in towns and cities where people are used to contact with people from the United States.

Useful words and phrases

English	Spanish
One	Uno
Two	Dos
Three	Tres
Four	Cuatro
Five	Cinco
Six	Seis
Seven	Siete
Eight	Ocho
Nine	Nueve
Ten	Diez
Sunday	Domingo
Monday	Lunes
Tuesday	Martes
Wednesday	Miércoles

Useful words and phrases

Thursday	Jueves
Friday	Viernes
Saturday	Sábado
Good morning	Buenos días
Good afternoon	Buenos tardes
Good night	Buenas noches
Goodbye	Adiós
Please	Por favor
Thank you	Gracias
Yes	Sí
No	No
Can you speak English?	Habla usted Inglés?
Excuse me	Perdóneme

INDEX

Acknowledgments
Book produced for Highlights for Children, Inc. by Bender Richardson White.
Editor: Lionel Bender
Designer and page make-up: Malcolm Smythe
Art Editor: Ben White
Editorial Assistant: Madeleine Samuel
Picture Researcher: Annabel Ossel
Production: Kim Richardson

Maps produced by Oxford Cartographers, England.
Banknotes from Thomas Cook Currency Services.
Stamps from Stanley Gibbons.
Reproduction work by MRM Graphics, England.

Editorial Consultant: Andrew Gutelle.
Guide to Mexico is approved by the Mexican Government Tourist Office, London.
Consultant: Carmen Garcia-Moreno, Mexico City
Managing Editor, Highlights New Products: Margie Hayes Richmond

Picture Credits
MGTO = Mexican Government Tourist Office, SAP = South American Pictures, TM = Tony Morrison, Z = Zefa.
t = top, b = bottom, l = left, r = right.
Cover: Z-Damm. Pages: 6: Z/H. Grathwohl. 6-7: Z/H. Sunak. 7: Z. 8: SAP/TM. 8-9: Z/J. Kuhnke. 9: Annabel Ossel. 10: SAP/TM. 10-11: SAP/TM. 11t: SAP/TM. 12b: Z-Damm. 12-13t: MGTO. 13: SAP/TM. 14:SAP/TM. 14-15: SAP/ Kimball Morrison. 15: Z. 16: SAP/TM. 17l: Z. 17r: SAP/TM. 18: SAP/TM. 18-19: MGTO. 19: Z/A. Boutin. 20: SAP/ TM. 21t: SAP/TM. 21b: SAP/TM. 22: Z/ H. Grathwohl. 22-23: SAP/Kimball Morrison. 23: SAP/Robert Francis. 24: SAP/Pedro Martinez. 25t: Z. 25b: SAP/TM. 26l: Z/Starfoto. 26l: MGTO. 27: SAP/TM. 28: Z/Boutin. 29: Z-Damm. 30: Z.
Map illustration on page 1 by Tom Powers